T0083560

THE LANTERN ROOM

THE
Lantern
Room

CHLOE HONUM

TUPELO PRESS
2022

ISBN-13: 978-1-946482-62-4
Identifiers: LCCN 2021014007 | ISBN 9781946482624
(paperback)
Subjects: LCGFT: Poetry.
Classification: LCC PS3608.O555 L36 2022 | DDC 811/.6--dc23
LC record available at https://lccn.loc.gov/2021014007

Cover and text design by adam b. bohannon.

First paperback edition January 2022.

Tupelo Press
P.O. Box 1767
North Adams, Massachusetts 01247
(413) 664-9611 / Fax: (413) 664-9711
editor@tupelopress.org / www.tupelopress.org

Tupelo Press is an award-winning independent literary
press that publishes fine fiction, non-fiction, and poetry in
books that are a joy to hold as well as read. Tupelo Press is
a registered 501(c)(3) non-profit organization, and we rely
on public support to carry out our mission of publishing
extraordinary work that may be outside the realm of the
large commercial publishers. Financial donations are
welcome and are tax deductible

This project is supported in part by an award from the
National Endowment for the Arts.

CONTENTS

I

LUNA MOTH AT NIGHT

The Angel

On the eve of my thirteenth birthday, I found her in an alley. Her wings were crossed at violent angles. She was naked and her bruises were so bright that I ran my finger along them to check if the skin was broken. I bathed and clothed her. The garment fell apart on her body, like silk floating down and severing itself on a sword. Since then, she has gone everywhere with me. Occasionally, people see her and startle. They ask her if she's all right, but she speaks only to me, as if I were the translator of her ancient, mottled language.

Luna Moth at Night

Pale green queen, in your fourth
and final form, you did not
come this far to be eaten.

In flight, the long tails
of your hindwings flutter, creating
the illusion of multiple targets.

Watching you, I wonder if writing
and erasing is one of my
creaturely instincts—

fingers darting,
sentences there, then gone,
the alphabet swept flat

by silence. You have fine veins
and maroon margins
on your broad front wings.

Your enemies are bats, owls,
and hornets. Mine are men
who lunged at my life

in both fast and slow motion.
You travel now how you must,
spinning phantoms.

I write *light, safe clearing, river,*
erase it, then write it again,
until it slips like a leaf into morning.

April in New England

Alone in my bedroom, I sob,
and the wardrobe steps forward,
like a coffin-mother, to embrace me.

Later, standing at the back door,
a coyote crosses my vision
on a wave of snow. What

is intimacy? Once, in a supermarket,
you slid up behind me,
covered my eyes, and said, *guess who?*

Did I recognize your touch or your voice?
I sleep with the windows open
and the rain climbs into my bed

like a lover, naked beneath the quilt.
I could roll over and wrap
my arms around the rain.

At the Dollar Save Inn in Magnolia, Arkansas

I stand in the doorway and the rain empties its hands into my hands.
　　The July wind plunges its hands into a rummage sale of heat.
The dogwood puts its hands behind its back and lowers its blossoming head.
　　The field can't read the green reminders written on its hand.
Sitting by the pool, painting her nails, a teenager blows on wet red moons
　　at the end of her hand. Across the street, by a gas station,
a man holds a cardboard sign that says *stranded* in a wobbly hand.
　　Dead sparrow on the concrete, this is not the place to wake
unnamable wants. Yet there you are, your feathers
　　rippling a little as the pink dusk changes hands.

Stopping by a Gas Station on
the Third Day of Driving Across the Country

When I close my eyes, I'm back in the dream, diving to the bottom
    of the lake in which he loved me. When I open my eyes, it's October
in Arkansas, in a brightly lit aisle of a Love's gas station. I concede:
    if silence is all he offers then I am thirsty for his silence.
Outside, the air is still and cold, with mist thickening in the trees.
    Pumping gas, feeling the handle pulse—who was he that even now
his silence gives the note I tune my voice to? Trucks shudder
    right through it, then clouds swoop low, tasseled with blackbirds.

Nightfall in Spring

Nightly, the smoke from the neighbor's incinerator pawed the air
    in our garden. Black flecks of newspaper settled
across the violets. From the tip of a twig, a praying mantis
    extended its lines, the green text of its body becoming an elegant,
indecipherable sentence, and with round green eyes looked out
    over the grass. Trumpet flowers exhaled mist. My mother crouched
in a white nightgown and cut sprigs of parsley and mint.
    She was addicted to downers, her mind a loom, its fabric the weather
of spring. The new leaves flickered like eyelids. Beneath the mailbox,
    wasps drew their plans for a nest—cloud-gray walls,
hexagon hollows. It was their night as much as it was ours.
    The dew on her feet. The shudder of their long, red wings.

Read More About Our History

In 1964, Maggie Wilkinson's daughter was taken from her after she gave birth at St. Mary's Home for unwed mothers, run by the Anglican Church in Ōtāhuhu, Auckland. She has pointed out that the history section of Auckland's Anglican Trust for Women and Children's website did not mention the home.

The history remembers twelve cows on average
    were milked, and that an Old Boy sent the secretary
a postcard from the Holy City. Maggie Wilkinson
    was told her records were lost in a fire— or a flood.
She was *force-fed drops (ergometrine)?... bound and given a drug to stop*
    lactation, stilbestoerol??? The history includes the names of many
Bishops and buildings, and the cost per annum of running things.
    Yet there is no space for the matron's soft shoes, her habit of
silently appearing behind Maggie and screaming if her mop strokes were not square.
    No room for the Bible on which the mothers were made to swear
never to try to find their children. Look at the rain tonight
    in Auckland, how insistently it searches, in hard spirals,
down Queen Street toward the sea. Winter has just begun.
    Soon, the moon will infuse the clouds with a color that has
no name— shy of silver, shy of violet. Homes of Compassion,
    some were called. St. Vincent's. St. Mary's. One girl,
in the weeks after giving birth, eased her ache by carrying
    the family cat in her arms *as one would a baby.*

St. Mary's Home for Unwed Mothers
in Ōtāhuhu, Auckland

a   constant danger—

people who desire

                    exceptional experience

in   controlling   girls

                    nature and scope of work

and   milk

Offerings

I have saved my pantomime of the sky for you. Let me lie with my head in your lap. I will sing the song of the trees in the cold wind, the way they rush up like flames, their leaves rippling. I want to show you everything you might have missed. With my fingers I will emulate moonlight resting on a field of violets. I am about as convincing as the child playing the sun in the school recital. But I have rain in my hair. This much is true. Let me bring it to you.

II

The Common Room

On the Stairs Outside the Psychiatric Ward

I stand with the boy with the injured body
while the smoke from his cigarette signs its slow signature.
He leans on his cane and the cane shakes.
It is late afternoon, almost dark.

We are day patients and soon will go home.
The boy says, *I got into some trouble in Texas*,
which is so far away it doesn't seem to exist,
not with what's going on now.

All around us autumn is throwing
gold and crimson leaves into the street
while starlings are holding tight on a telephone wire,
heads tucked in the cold. And the boy

and the Vietnam vet, who has just joined us,
and I are looking up with yearning, as though
we could solve that string of bird and sky arithmetic
and know the ages of our souls.

Stairway

The windows in the common room look down on a parking lot. Snow keeps coming, though it is already the conqueror of anything it wants. When a baby is born, a speaker mounted above the hospital entrance plays a lullaby. One patient wonders aloud why music doesn't play when somebody dies, suggests "Stairway to Heaven." On my drive home, trucks swallow the narrow hills. I all but close my eyes. Hurry, darling. I would side with winter—if it would free me, I would stay.

Lunch Break in the Day Patient Ward

The fluorescent light is covering me like a hood of silk. It smells of sweat and medicine. The fish tank in the hallway is a risk and a gesture. A box of wonder—we are trusted not to throw ourselves against it.

*

Once, when I was small, my mother lay on the carpet and asked me to walk barefoot up her back. I grew very light, hovering above myself, and made the journey. I had to balance my distance from her body. When she rolled over, my feet became birds in the golden leaves of her hair.

*

Outside, the boy with the injured body is leaning on his cane and smoking a cigarette. The sky, the snow, and the smoke pass gray, white, and silver around in a circle. In an hour, we will go back inside the building. We'll climb the narrow stairs, as if venturing into the attics of our lives.

Stay Beside Me

The psychiatric ward has three levels. We are the day patients, and above us are the overnighters. Above them are those in the most danger. In the common room, the Vietnam vet tells me that his father, the police chief, molested his sisters. When he says, *my sisters*, his slow, gravelly voice rises. Then he falls silent. I think he is afraid to be womanly. But in the shade beneath his ball cap, the word *sisters* keeps rising, like the moon above a beach where dolphins have mistaken its light for a shared mind, and are swimming in with the waves.

The Ward Above

I don't need to look up to know that inside some of the fluorescent lights there are dead flies on their backs, their wings at crisp diagonals. The psychiatrist has a face like an old dictionary. I imagine myself in the ward above, for the more severe cases. I'm afraid I'll float up and ask to be admitted. In the common room, the Vietnam vet says, *No, you don't want to go up there*. Everything he says, he says again with his eyes. At home, my dog sleeps beside me. She groans as I slide my hand beneath her head. I speak to her. I carry her warm, happy skull through the night.

Late Afternoon with Geese

The counselor plays his game of questions.
If you could live in any time period,
he asks us, *when would you live?*

Now, the manic boy answers, as though jumping
to the head of the queue to enter the present.
Not now, the Vietnam vet says,

it's too violent, and he talks about the late
Fifties, the Friday nights
dancing at the Showboat.

Outside, the rain comes to a feathery end.
The geese introduce themselves to dusk
with ragged cries. Winter at their backs,

they heave upward.
Their wings open like old, heavy books,
their stories veering into the wild.

Late Afternoon with Waterfall

The fluorescent light
goes off and the shadows
fall apart like a cardboard fort.

The invisible should be sturdier,
like that stormy summer
the rain came so heavy

the waterfall was just
a thicker column of sky.
Now a fly throws itself

down on the formica table
and buzzes and spins
on its back, quickening

the poison. It resembles
a word scribbled out.
Won't do, won't do.

But oh you of the river-
wet lips, I miss you
this moment, and this.

We're Supposed to Get Snow Tonight

One patient among us has had shock therapy. I ask if it helped and she shrugs both shoulders. Staring at the floor, she says, *I think it does affect the memory*. One patient wears the softest clothes. Even her boots are soft. She says, *It's a good day if I get to see him*, as she drifts across the room. During our lunch break, I drive into town. The hills roll fast then slow, keeping pace with a crow arcing overhead. I buy a latte, wrap my hands around the paper cup, and hold still for a moment on the sidewalk. Coming toward me, a hooded woman carries a gladiola like a spine in bloom. She passes without raising her eyes. And the wind grows colder.

Late Morning with Blossoms

One patient among us suspects we are actors in a play. He is a gentle interrogator, and moves slowly around the common room. Between questions, he folds and refolds his handkerchief. I have seen his face before in heavy, browning blossoms, ancient and disorganized. The counselor asks, *And you, too? Are you also an actor?* The man nods then shakes his head. His eyes are apologetic. Beyond the window, there's a pause in the rain. Something shimmering and tear-streaked begins to turn, though whether it's coming or leaving we can't say.

Group Therapy

The counselor is passing around a black, velvet sack filled with questions. *What is your idea of a perfect evening? Who is your biggest inspiration?* He's beaming, waiting for our answers. Beyond the window, autumn toys with ideas of heaven. The trees become fiercely talented and focused. Then winter.

*

Some say love, it is a river, I sang as a girl in school assembly. We sang standing up. I was ready to faint all that year. For five days each month, my blood came as bright as plum juice. When I finally fainted, it was as silky as I'd imagined, as if sleeping and waking were two sides of one pearl.

*

In any group, I want to know: Who's the mother? The boy with the injured body, he's the angel. The Vietnam vet is the son. The nervous old lady is the baby. The counselor is the meddling neighbor. Now that I see a family, I can breathe. The leaves are crimson. I have something to tear down.

Before Group Meditation

I recall splendor.
On a borrowed bicycle,
I wobbled fast

downhill over jutting roots,
a swarm of horseflies
like a grainy moon

following close behind.
At the bottom of the hill:
a little rain shining in

a corner of wind.
Now the upbeat counselor
passes around a basket

of rocks. My friend,
the Vietnam vet, says,
I knew I wasn't going to be smart

so boy I was going to be tough.
All his sentences are like that,
clean as autumn. Each afternoon

we sit in a circle. I take a rock,
I wish you were here,
and I pass the basket on.

The Master of Dreams

By late afternoon, the master of dreams
is close beside me. I hand him his props.
I give him my scarf, the clingy texture

of a hibiscus, and pass him a ringing
phone that I don't want to answer.
Sometimes he takes things on his own.

In the common room, I drop an apple
and the master of dreams whisks it away
on a river of fluorescent light. Silent

and meticulous, he takes notes on the wind
and the falling crimson leaves. By evening
he waits in a shimmering boat.

He comes from a place both deeper
and closer than Nowhere,
though he has lived Nowhere, too.

Noon with Miracle Drugs

First one psychiatrist is gone, pulled away
on a tide of fluorescent light.
Then the other is gone, too,
to tend to matters in the ward above.

In the common room, we talk about side effects,
night sweats and low libidos,
and about miracle drugs. *Like a light switch*,
the girl in the soft boots says, and we look longingly

beyond the window, at the birds
draped like strings of black pearls
around the saffron-colored trees.
The man who thinks we're actors in a play

asks me questions about poetry.
Flowers freshly cut and wrapped in newspaper,
that's how I want to rest, my dreams
like white petals absorbing ink.

Note Home

Mother, you have never seen such snow, such insistence on setting. So it is accurate to say my heart broke in the snow. One patient here is a Vietnam vet. His torso is hard like an old-fashioned suit-case. *Kick my dog,* he said today, referring to his beloved animal over ten years dead, *and I'll kick your ass.* The light is slippery. Everything hums. It is so important to go on naming, even if all I said to you this winter was *snow, snow, snow.*

Late Afternoon with Kiwi and Sky

The fluorescent light
in the group therapy room
is vetting me for some

terrible migration.
I ask the counselor
to turn it off.

My native bird
is flightless. It's a
cousin to the moa,

a walking hut of a bird.
The light goes off
and suddenly

it's late afternoon
and cloudy. I listen
to the voices of my new

friends who I
will never see again.
My native bird

is nocturnal.
Though it has lived
millions of years,

it and the sky have
reached
no agreement.

The Lighthouse

In the day patient ward, between lunch and the next activity, the man who thinks we're actors in a play recites a poem. *She lived near here*, he says about the poet, nodding toward the gray hills slick with rain. I almost tell him that I am living in her house, among her books and paintings, but decide it could sound too strange. Across the table, the Vietnam vet is remembering a friend who lost two sons to suicide, one, then a few months later, the other. *Dear God*, someone softly says. We shake our heads and drink our water, coffee, or tea from little Styrofoam cups. There are vision boards displayed along one wall. Glancing at them, I think that if the counselor brings in magazines, scissors, and glue, I'll sit it out. Too cheesy, I tell myself, too juvenile. But that's not it. I sip my water. Empty, the cup is so light it's hard to hold. The vision boards are pinned edge to edge, a series of raw hope. I can barely look at them, knowing I too might choose the daisy, the word *joy* in royal blue, or the lighthouse, cutting shakily up the side of the tower and around the lantern room.

Phoebe

At the clinic, a nurse taps my veins and they find their tiny voices. Blood sweeps into the vial and a chunk of snow slides from my boot. The shine on the linoleum floor is brutal, but no one is saying so. Outside, it is both noon and evening, as if winter were trying to be giving. In the parking lot: a hooded woman. You want to know what I believe? I believe my dog would come between my death and me, that she would come huffing and shaking all over, as her dreams allow.

New England Lyric

In group, when the counselor sets a big pad of paper
on an easel at the front of the room
and asks each of us to write

an inspiring quote or lyric,
I go with *All you need is love*,
which I think of as

a question, a true or false.
Don't worry, be happy,
writes the smiley young teacher

whose meds are dangerously off.
And the Vietnam vet offers
Take this job and shove it,

which he swears is one of the best
sentences he's ever spoken.
O steep, gray hills of New England.

O teenager balling up his apron
mid-shift on a Friday night so he could go
dancing at the Showboat.

O early spring—the stiff mud
that makes a fleshy sound
as I run through it at dusk,

afraid of my voice, its new
slipperiness with words, echoes, windows.
O cold, dicey blooms.

The Dreams

The trouble with that one, someone says about a certain medication, *was the dreams*. A few of us nod, as though *the dreams* are a city we too have visited. With some it is dry mouth. Or a metallic taste. Or quickened speech. And with this one, we agree, comes dreams; the Vietnam vet gives a low whistle to indicate their intensity. Then the talk turns to dogs we love, or have loved and dearly miss. Then to the rain falling in dense violet streaks. These are the unsupervised moments, the in-between. It is morning. We are waiting. Spring is coming—officially, it is already here. I spread my hand like a wing to show my trembling pinky.

What I'm Working on Now

The title is Survive This

The title is Whispered into My Hands

The title is Blue Hills, Blue Rain

The title is In the Winter to End All Winters

The title is Phoebe of New England

The title is Laughter in the Psychiatric Ward

The title is The Quiet of the Man Who Thinks We're Actors in a
  Play

The title is I Remember the Showboat

The title is Don't Write About the Moon

The title is Moon

The title is Hey, Doc

The title is Don't Be Afraid

The title is O My Enemy

The title is Listen, Buddy

The title is White Bread Sandwiches

The title is Little Styrofoam Cup of Water

The title is Stories from the Ward Above

The title is My New Friends Who I Will Never See Again

The title is Tentative

The title is Unexpected Side Effect

The title is I Pissed on His Grave and That's Not a Figure of
  Speech Either

The title is Soft Boots

The title is Violins at Dusk

The title is You Can't Always Get What You Want, But If You Try
  Sometimes. . . .

The title is Trailing Off
The title is Take a Rock
The title is Close Your Eyes
The title is Breathless
The title is Blue Hills, Blue Lightning
The title is Ten Years of Translating Thunder
The title is Intake Questions About Joy
The title is Joy
The title is Center Stage and Mumbling
The title is A Totally Erased Poem
The title is Whirling Gods
The title is The Coyote's Ribs
The title is Straggly Morning Choir
The title is Moth Haloed
The title is Sobbing
The title is Hello, You're Late
The title is Sudsy White Blossoms, Indigo Sky
The title is The Inevitability of Spring
The title is Intermission
The title is Ellipsis
The title is How to Get There
The title is Tumble, Leap
The title is Follow the Dog Running in Her Dream

III

SELF-PORTRAIT
WITH PRAYING MANTIS

At Americas Best Value Inn in Crossett, Arkansas

Mist turns rain turns mist again. The cusp of summer. Sparrows
    sing the night in question into question. Maybe sense is not a place
I want to linger, like the concrete hallway that leads to the ice machine,
    the ground studded with old chewing gum. By my feet, two
        butterflies twirl
like fire that has lost its way. I find my room and close the door,
    a beige door bearing a stranger's—or many strangers'—inky
        fingerprints.
In the morning: a cool wind, the treetops tracing the letters of their
    private alphabet.
    In the distance: white clots of smoke rising from the Georgia-Pacific
        paper plant.
All those hot blank pages—who needs them? My phone could ring
    at any moment. You could say _____. Mother Silence
could appear behind me, waving from any one of these dark windows.

Love Is a Wound that Will Happen

The motel is from another era, its horseshoe driveway a half-loop of
    time.
   The wind beats the hills like carpets and orange pollen
tumbles down. I wish you could show me again the black and white
    picture of your mother playing Juliet in Florence, the sleeves of her
       dress
flaring like trumpet flowers. It's summer. The stars come out;
    in what tense they shine, I've never been clear. Shutting my eyes,
pulling the rough white sheet to my chin, I listen to the sparrows
    closing the trees, someone laughing, and in the leaves the rain
      picking up
exactly where it left off eight years ago one August morning.

At Scull Creek in Fayetteville, Arkansas

Moments after the sky declares the rain absent,
 it begins falling roughly through the leaves. I miss you,
and worse, I want to say it the way another poet would.
 The creek is green-gold, the water moving
around stones and slabs of concrete. I walk loudly
 through it, feel it wrap around my ankles. Last night,
at a motel in Sallisaw, I watched a row of pale blue doors
 lean into sunset, like words in an aching sentence.
My shame is that I didn't believe you, not fully. Beneath
 the rippling surface, there's stillness, clear and cold,
where tiny glinting fish form patterns only to dissolve them.

Motel with Storm and Map

On the outskirts of a thundering town,
I checked in. My hair was swingy with rain,
my umbrella blown inside out.
The concrete stairs went up and up;

had they risen one flight higher
I might have slept in a palace of violet
and silver clouds. As it was, my room
was an ugly place to miss you from,

with thin carpet and curtains
that seemed to exhale dust.
Seeing myself in the speckled mirror,
I lay flat on the bed. In my hand was a map

on which the clerk had circled
my home for the night—
among a series of doors,
a blurry number inside a drop of rain.

Europe

Once, on a too hot bus, my sister and I traveled through fields of
    sunflowers.
Because we couldn't stop arguing, we sat rows apart.
I see us staring out the windows. Or eating the food we took
from the motel breakfast. Bread rolls wrapped in napkins.
Little tubs of yogurt. I see us washing our hands
in the thin stream of water in the bus's lavatory.
Wanting to apologize, but too embarrassed of our inability
to protect or soothe the other. Far away, our mother had died,
though we didn't know it. Our grandmother, rightly afraid
of how we'd bear the news, waited until we returned to tell us.
I was seventeen and my sister was twenty. I see us writing postcards
from Florence and Capri. *Today I swam in the Emerald Grotto* . . .
Our handwriting wobbly from the vibrations of the bus—
gaps and smudges where one pen ran dry and another began,
drowsy hearts beneath our names.

At a Days Inn in Barstow, California

It's dusk on a Tuesday in June. A hot wind
    bears down and east. In my room, a stranger's
hairclip lies like a gilded insect beside the sink.
    Hours later, it's still dusk. Last month,
I cut the masking tape from a box my mother left
    my sister and me. On the lid, she wrote, *Life is hard, <u>not</u>*
unbeatable. If I can do it, darlings, so can you. 2 AM. A rosy dark
    dusting the window, the heat a ladder into sleep.

Birthday at a Motel 6

The summer rain takes one last sweep through the leaves.
　　Sunlight shimmers on the stones below. In the parking lot,
two girls smoke as they stroll, following the gray scrolls of their breath.
　　Some of the doors are open to dim rectangular scenes
as intricate as tarot cards—Lovers and Fools and High Priestesses.
　　Above them the wind carries petals over dusk's border.
Sparrows hunt for their inheritance in the trampled grass.
　　And my question endures another year, lit by tiny stars
striking out across Arkansas. How will I live without her?

Elegy with Cannons and Bees

Auckland, 2019

It rained all night and still is not over.
Nevertheless, the bees
throw themselves roughly

into autumn.
What happened?
Why did you have to go?

In Albert Park,
water arcs continuously
from cherubs' horns.

Painted cannons
face the city.
I am no closer to knowing

and it will be twenty-one
years in July.
The light is tightening.

Nevertheless, all day
the bees glow
gold in the gloom,

working up and down
an ivy-covered brick wall,
as if trying to lift it.

Document

Large rat in the courtyard of the Auckland Art Gallery,
in daylight, what are you after? People walking by
have varying reactions to you. Some make faces of dislike.
One boy smiles and pauses awhile to watch you.
Others look at you and away with no change
in expression. You scurry alongside your reflection
in a wall of glass, stopping and starting unnervingly,
then turn and hop easily up the stairs.
Your eyes are gentle, even hopeful, in their way.
Yet you make me shiver. When you hold still, your tail
lies flat behind you, a dark line on the smooth concrete.
Like a place to sign at the end of an old, unreadable year.

At the Garden Inn in Blytheville, Arkansas

It seems right that summer
should lead to this:
a low brick structure

and a row of violet doors
covered in dust. Above wet
steamy grass, a butterfly lifts

the sky on its powdery wings.
In my room, I check the mattress
for bugs, pull the creases taut

to examine flecks of tobacco
and dirt. Lying down,
head in sunlight, body in shadow,

I dream of you again—
it's becoming chronic—
but wake thinking *Blytheville*,

like a silky claw reaching in
to remind me where I am.
July in Blytheville, in a season

governed—*if it be sweet,*
if it be not sweet—
by warm, pushy rain.

Teaching Poetry at the Juvenile Detention Center
in Fayetteville, Arkansas

It's cold and the light is blurry,
the fluorescents spasming,
the walls a steely gray.
Each child is given a pencil.

Their cells are just beyond
the heavy sliding doors.
They write get-away poems
and treehouse poems.

Sack of weed and siren poems.
A flea appears on my arm
and quivers, like a fleck of onyx.
I watch it bite and gleam, and the boys

sitting across from me
watch it, too. In a concrete
tomb, hope is anything
that travels in big leaps.

Self-Portrait with Praying Mantis and Rain

In the wet heat of June, the flies are declaring triumph.
    Mulberries have fallen all over the porch and are turning quickly
into mush with a bright, sour scent. Whatever the praying mantis wants,
    whatever vision she is conjuring from her place of stillness on the
        railing,
I want to lie down tonight and surrender to it. (I loved you, I'm sorry,
    is how I expect it will go, but who knows now that her wings have
        snapped open
and she has flown in a clean arc into the first wave of blue rain.)
    The birds have started to shriek and the trees to sway in wide circles,
all their leaves raised. What I mean to say, whatever else
    in those years was true, in Arkansas, in the wet heat
(red wings, green wings), as much as I did anything, I dreamt of you.

Self-Portrait with Praying Mantis and Endurance

All summer, my dreams have let in rain, finding endless uses
    for the sound of wet leaves rubbing together. At dawn,
I step onto the porch and watch spiders milling about
    in their webs; sometimes they spin them inside my mailbox,
so I reach my hand in and feel, instead of emptiness, their sticky silk.
    Hours turn like pages, moving a plot deeper into heat,
filled with petals and fleas and, now and then,
    a praying mantis, which strikes me as a model of dignity,
with its big green stillness, like a mind that will not be sent scuttling
    into the past. *Extend the lines of the body*, my ballet teacher
would say, but that was long ago, and I am trying to stay here among
    the storms, dust, and hardy plants. Hairy, bee-addled wisteria.
Papery discs of lunaria— also called moonwort, silver dollar, honesty.

NOTES

"The Angel" is after "Man and Camel" by Mark Strand.

"Stopping by a Gas Station on the Third Day of Driving Across the Country" is after "Fish and Watergrass" by Henri Cole.

The italicized language in "Read More About Our History" is drawn from supporting articles and letters included in Petition 2014/80: Inquiry into Misuse of the Adoption Act, submitted by Maggie Wilkinson to the New Zealand Parliament in 2016. Wilkinson called for the House to undertake an inquiry into the practice of "forced adoption" in New Zealand during the 1950s to the 1980s.

"St. Mary's Home for Unwed Mothers in Ōtāhuhu, Auckland" is an erasure poem drawn from the former text of the history section of the Auckland Anglican Trust for Women and Children's website.

The title "Love Is a Wound that Will Happen" is taken from a line in the poem "The Poinsettias" by Thomas James.

The italicized language in the final stanza of "At the Garden Inn in Blytheville, Arkansas" is taken from the poem "Rowing" by Anne Sexton.

"Self-Portrait with Praying Mantis and Rain" is after "Pillowcase with Praying Mantis" by Henri Cole.

A NOTE TO READERS

The poems in this collection are narrated by a speaker who is not
identical to myself. As in a play or a novel, the figures, settings, and
situations represented are not inherently nonfiction or autobiog-
raphy but rather may draw from archetype and imagination.

ACKNOWLEDGEMENTS

My gratitude to the editors of the following publications, in which these poems, sometimes in earlier forms, first appeared. Poems from this collection also appeared in a chapbook, *Then Winter,* published by Bull City Press as an editors' selection from the 2016 Frost Place Chapbook Competition.

32 Poems: "Motel with Storm and Map" (as "The Motel")

Academy of American Poets Poem-a-Day: "At a Days Inn in Barstow, California"

Adroit Journal: "Document"

Alaska Quarterly Review: "Noon with Miracle Drugs" (as "Rest"); "The Lighthouse," and "The Dreams" (as "The Common Room")

American Literary Review: "Nightfall in Spring"

Blackbird: "Love Is a Wound that Will Happen" and "Stopping at a Gas Station on the Third Day of Driving Across the Country"

Copper Nickel: "The Ward Above"

Crazyhorse: "The Master of Dreams" (as "Exhaustion in the Psychiatric Ward")

Day One: "Late Morning with Blossoms" (as "Blossoms in the Psychiatric Ward")

Diode: "At Americas Best Value Inn in Crossett, Arkansas" and "Teaching Poetry at the Juvenile Detention Center in Fayetteville, Arkansas"

Gulf Coast: "Self-Portrait with Praying Mantis and Rain"

Harvard Review Online: "On the Stairs Outside the Psychiatric
    Ward"
Hotel Amerika: "Stairway" (as "First Day of Partial
    Hospitalization,") "Note Home," and "We're Supposed to Get
    Snow Tonight"
Linebreak: "Offerings"
Nashville Review: "At Scull Creek in Fayetteville, Arkansas"
One Throne: "Late Afternoon with Kiwi and Sky" (as "Kiwi")
Orion: "At the Dollar Save Inn in Magnolia, Arkansas"
Raleigh Review: "At the Garden Inn in Blytheville, Arkansas,"
    "Birthday at a Motel 6"
Salamander: "Phoebe"
The Southern Review: "The Angel," "Before Group Meditation" (as
    "Before Group Meditation in the Psychiatric Ward"), "Read
    More About Our History," and "St. Mary's Home for Unwed
    Mothers in Otahuhu, Auckland"
The Spinoff: "Elegy with Cannons and Bees"
storySouth: "Late Afternoon with Geese" (as "Early Winter in the
    Psychiatric Ward")
Tupelo Quarterly: "Luna Moth at Night," "New England Lyric,"
    "Self-Portrait with Praying Mantis and Endurance" and
    "What I'm Working on Now"
Two Peach: "April in New England" (as "Breakdown in April")
    and "Stay Beside Me"
The Volta: "Late Afternoon with Waterfall" (as "Late Afternoon in
    the Psychiatric Ward")
Waxwing: "Group Therapy" (as "Group Therapy in the
    Psychiatric Ward") and "Lunch Break in the Day Patient
    Ward" (as "Lunch Break in the Psychiatric Ward")

For their friendship and support, my deep thanks to Judith Bingyou, Betsy Bonner, Lisa Fay Coutley, Mag Gabbert, Rebecca Gayle Howell, Meaghan Mulholland, Emily Pulfer-Terino, Shellie Shores, Lisa Russ Spaar, Ariadne Thompson, and Rosemary Wages.

Thank you to my family in the U.S. and in New Zealand.

Thank you to Kristina Marie Darling, David Rossitter, adam b. bohannon, Jeffrey Levine, and everyone at Tupelo Press for their faith in this book.

Thank you to Baylor University, especially my wonderful colleagues in the English department.

Thank you to the Grimshaw Sargeson Fellowship in Auckland for your generosity and hospitality and for four beautiful months in the city of my youth.

To Jacob Shores-Argüello and to Phoebe, bright and shining, all my love.